SELECTED POEMS

Wesleyan Poetry

Selected Poems
Harvey Shapiro

With an Introduction by James Atlas

Wesleyan University Press
Published by University Press of New England
Hanover and London

Wesleyan University Press
Published by University Press of New England, Hanover, NH 03755

© 1997 by Harvey Shapiro
Simultaneously published by
Carcanet Press Limited
Manchester, England

Printed in Great Britain 5 4 3 2 1

CIP data appear at the end of the book

Contents

Acknowledgments

Selected poems from Harvey Shapiro's *National Cold Storage Company* © 1988 by Wesleyan University Press by permission, University Press of New England.

Selected poems from Harvey Shapiro's *The Light Holds* © 1984 by Wesleyan University Press by permission, University Press of New England.

Other poems are from *Lauds & Nightsounds* © 1978 by SUN, and *A Day's Portion* © 1994 by Hanging Loose Press.

My thanks to those publishers and to the following magazines: *Poetry East, Poetry New York, The Jewish Quarterly, Boulevard, Hanging Loose*. The poems 'Prague', 'History', and 'In Tiberius' are reprinted from *Prairie Schooner* by permission of the University of Nebraska Press. The poems 'The Ticket' and 'Italy' appeared in *The New Yorker*.

Introduction

I remember vividly my first encounter with Harvey Shapiro. I was twenty-five, living in Cambridge and working on my first book, a biography of Delmore Schwartz, and I would go down to New York periodically to interview Delmore's colleagues and friends, people who had known Delmore and could offer me their living testimony. Someone – I can't remember who now – suggested I go see this poet who worked as an editor at the *New York Times Magazine* and had known Delmore in the 1940s and 1950s. I was excited. I was familiar with Shapiro's work; I had one of his books, *Battle Report*, on my shelf. I'd read it in high school, when I myself still had dreams of becoming a poet, in the series of books put out by Wesleyan University Press. They were austere and handsome books, the poems on large wide pages enveloped by white space – as if to convey that poetry was a demanding trade, unadorned by literary finery. Robert Bly's first collection was in that series, and some of James Wright's early books. They moved me, but it was in Shapiro's poems that I heard the voice of my own Jewish ancestors, a voice drenched in what Shapiro has defined as his 'tribal identity' – father-haunted, Holocaust-obsessed, longing for a place in the world:

> *And this is law, or so is said*
> *Within the darkening synagogue*
> *By old men, honored in their beards*
> *By the unsealed, heroic sounds,*
> *Celebration without end, the dark book*
> *Whispers to the wind,*
> *Wind cradles the destructive globe.*

Shapiro's language, like Delmore's, claimed for poetry the particular experience of my people, who had come to America at the turn of the century as part of the great Jewish immigration from Eastern Europe and made their uneasy home in America. Shapiro was their child; I was their grandchild.

But if this poetry spoke to me in a voice I could under-
stand, there was nothing provincial about it. Shapiro was a
'native of Chicago', according to his author's note (this detail,
too, touched me, another Chicago boy); but he'd grown up in
New York and gone to Yale. He had also fought in World War
II; at the age of nineteen, he was a radio gunner with the
Fifteenth Air Force. He'd flown thirty-five missions over Ger-
many and Austria in a B-17. (How unimaginable to a child of
the Vietnam era, for whom war was a thing to be avoided.)
In 'Battle Report', Shapiro produced one of the great poems
to come out of the war – like Randall Jarrell's brief classic,
'The Death of the Ball Turret Gunner', like the great war
poems of Wilfred Owen and Edward Thomas, a poem that
made combat the occasion for reflections on the transience
of being. His experience in the war had induced 'some clari-
fying chill', as Shapiro later put it.

What I admired about his poems was the way they blended
the forms and cadences of English literature with an urban
idiom that was entirely his own. 'I see myself following my
father's ghost through the streets of New York City,' he once
said, 'beset like him by the same dislocation, the same cul-
tural shock.' There was a directness to his work that gave it
immediacy, the sense of a man observing himself less in
self-consciousness than in wonder at the convergence of
unfathomable events – of birth, history, and temperament –
that had brought him to this moment. 'And all the structures
of my language lie undone' – in fact, it was Shapiro's language
that gave structure to his life.

I went to the offices of the *New York Times* on West 43rd
Street, in gritty Times Square, and called him up. The maga-
zine was in a big, gloomy room on the eighth floor. The walls
were hospital green; the floor was linoleum; there was
chicken wire on the dirty windows. 'It was a time of green
eyeshades and wooden desks,' Shapiro recalled. He greeted
me and led me over to his desk (in my memory, not wooden
but metal). He was slight, bearded, somewhat shy, but hardly
ethereal; it was the middle of the working day, and editors
were hurrying back and forth. Phones – black rotary-dial
phones – were ringing. (They went largely unanswered in

those days.) I don't recall much of our conversation; it was mostly about Delmore's poetry, and its influence on Shapiro's generation. But I was struck by how in-the-world he was, how comfortable in the midst of the urgent activity going on around him. Poetry, it seemed, could co-exist with daily life – what Lionel Trilling, in a memorable phrase, once called 'the hum and buzz of implication'.

One of the more curious developments in recent American poetry has been its specialization. Wallace Stevens in his insurance office, Eliot at his bank, gave way in the post-war years to the poet as academic, on a tenure track or teaching in one of the writing programs that proliferated on campuses across the country, granting poets an MFA (Master of Fine Arts) so that they in turn could teach other poets the poetry business, the poetry game. Even the poets of the so-called Tragic Generation – Delmore, Jarrell, John Berryman, Robert Lowell – ended up in front of a classroom. The more marginal the poet became, the more exalted his status – 'the poet as priest', as Shapiro described this view of his vocation in an illuminating interview with the American poet Michael Heller.

But 'you can't be a priest in a newspaper office,' he noted tartly. Editing copy, he told Heller, was useful for a poet; moving paragraphs around, penciling in changes, finding the lead made him more at home with words. 'My job has never been an easy job.' No, but it enabled him, I suspect, to get into poetry the 'flatfooted anti-heroic, fumbling, Yiddish-English' that he had responded to in the poetry of Delmore Schwartz. Shapiro's later poetry is rough-hewn, coarse, even at times pornographic. The lessons of the Objectivists whose work he studied so closely in his formative years – George Oppen, Louis Zukofsky, Charles Reznikoff – is still evident in his formal imagery; but so is the raw confessional verve of Allen Ginsberg. The late poems (and Shapiro has been writing long enough, with enough variety, to warrant the temporal division accorded Yeats and other poets whose work constitutes an *oeuvre*) open out; they're confident, jazzy, energized by the demotic: 'As you watch from the bed,/ the women rise in their glory/ to go to the john.' There's nothing academic here; sex, booze, the neon glow of late nights in a bar: these are Shapiro's territory. If his work hasn't achieved the recognition some of his contemporaries enjoy, if he belongs to no identifiable 'school', his independence has in some ways been a blessing. In one óf the biographical entries on his work, he quotes a phrase from Emily Dickinson – 'The sailor cannot see the North, but knows the needle can' – and observes: 'Just so, I have always trusted the poems to find their direction.' And they have.

For so many American poets active now, writing is a willed enterprise; young writers speak of wanting to be poets rather than of wanting to write poetry. In the life and work of Harvey Shapiro you feel a rare unity. He has lived in the same place, Brooklyn Heights, for nearly his entire writing life; he has immersed himself in the rituals of his own neighbourhood with an almost religious intensity. For Shapiro, as David Ray noted in a review of *The Light Holds*, poetry is 'a vehicle for redemption and understanding'. On the streets of Brooklyn and Queens, on the promenade overlooking Manhattan, on Houston Street, 'the moon coming up over Katz's delicatessen', he concentrates a unique purity of vision on the features of his own life. The opening lines of 'Traveling Through Ireland' are emblematic:

> Sitting beside a sign
> pointing to Cork and Limerick
> or in Irish *Corcaigh*
> and *Luimneach*,
> I am persuaded again
> of my foreignness in this world,
> and that none of the signs I read
> points to happiness. And
> many I can't make out.
> Though this world is the only world
> it is composed of infinite worlds.
> In one of them, I take
> my rightful place.

When I come into the office now – I, too, work at the *New York Times Magazine* – I look in on Harvey in the tiny private annex, a room with his own door, bestowed on him after forty years on the paper. The big room where the rest of us work is carpeted now, and we sit in burlap-walled carrels with computers and complicated phones; the ceilings are white cork, the lighting bright. ('I have always led a bourgeois life,' he told Michael Heller. 'By choice not by chance.') What hasn't changed is the view from the smudged chicken-wire windows, the rooftops and tall office towers of a city that I see freshly now because of Harvey Shapiro's poetry. Comforted by his presence, I recall these lines:

> I am on the lookout for
> A great illumining,
> Prepared to recognize it
> Instantly and put it to use
> Even among the desks
> And chairs of the office, should
> It come between nine and five.

JAMES ATLAS

The Heart

In the midst of words your wordless image
Marches through the precincts of my night
And all the structures of my language lie undone:
The bright cathedrals clatter, and the moon-
Topped spires break their stalk.
Sprawled before that raid, I watch the towns
Go under. And in the waiting dark, I loose
Like marbles spinning from a child
The crazed and hooded creatures of the heart.

Summer

The glazed day crumbles to its fall
Upon the tiny rout of fishing
Boats. Gulls convey it down,
Lengthening their cries that soon
Will rake the evening air; while some,
Silhouetted on a strand
In a jumbled line of target ducks,
Watch as ebb tide drains the bay.

From a rotted log upon
The shore, like the other beached
Mutations, shell and weed, I wait
For Highland Light to cast its eye.

July unhives its heaven in
A swarm of stars above my head.
And at my feet, flat to the water
That it rides, the lighthouse beam,
A broken spar, breaks its pulse.

'What have I learned of word or line?'
Ticks on, ticks off; ticks on, ticks off.
The bay, that was a clotted eye,
Is turned to water by the dark.
Only my summer breaks upon
The sea, the gulls, the narrow land.

Power in America

The struck animal, blurred
By subsequent hours, lies
Upon the road, hunched fur and spirit.
At night, drawn by the hum of power
Then doubled into pain, sight smashed,
It caught the radicals of
Descending speed, their brilliance.

Or the boy in Dreiser's novel,
That blind head, felled
By the big city hotel,
Its monolithic shine and scramble.
Even Crane, who tried to make
A shining steel structure of a bridge
Lead him out, caught by the brilliance
That kills, in America.

As at the movie's close,
Man alone, against the wall,
Watches the lights move in,
The fugitive, hatless there.
And we, thrilled into our fear,
See the enormously wheeled clatter,
Glistening, never in error,
Rise to break his back.

Death of a Grandmother

Let me borrow her corpse a little.
Over that clown in finest linen,
Over that white-dressed dummy, pretty girl
(Dressed for a party, the daughters cried),
Let me speak a line.

The dead lie in a ditch of fear,
In an earth wound, in an old mouth
That has sucked them there.
My grandmother drank tea, and wailed
As if the Wailing Wall kissed her head
Beside the kitchen window;
While the flaking, green-boxed radio
Retailed in Yiddish song
And heartache all day long.
Or laughter found her,
The sly, sexual humour of the grave.

Yet after her years of dragging leg,
Of yellowed sight,
She still found pain enough
To polish off the final hours with a shriek.
To what sweet kingdom do the old Jews go?
Now mourned by her radio and bed,
She wishes me health and children,
Who am her inheritor.

I sing her a song of praise.
She meddled with my childhood
Like a witch, and I can meet her
Curse for curse in that slum heaven where we go
When this American dream is spent –
To give her a crust of bread, a little love.

Adoration of the Moon

for Max Weber

Sappho's moist lotus and the scudding moon
Speak to each other in a dilation upon Acheron.
Lean out of the abyss of origin four ragged Jews,
Masters of wrath and judgment, gentled by the moon.
Their tall hats rise, their faces lengthen
As O the spell is on them. Three grip
The word for ballast, while the fourth,
Beard upended, sniffs the moon-fleck as it falls.
Support them in flight, goddess,
That when the darkness comes, thy light put out,
Their candle's flame send up in steep aroma
The scholar's must.

The Talker

from a midrash

While all the choiring angels cried:
Creation's crown is set awry!
God fabled man before he was,
And boasting of His enterprise
Bade angels say the simple names
That mark in place each bird and beast.

But they were dumb, as He foretold –
When man stepped from the shuddering dust
And lightly tossed the syllables,
And said his own name, quick as dirt.
Then angels crept into their spheres,
And dirt, and bird, and beast were his.

Mountain, Fire, Thornbush

How everything gets tamed.
The pronominal outcry, as if uttered in ecstasy,
Is turned to syntax. We are
Only a step from discursive prose
When the voice speaks from the thornbush.
Mountain, fire, and thornbush.
Supplied only with these, even that aniconic Jew
Could spell mystery. But there must be
Narrative. The people must get to the mountain.
Doors must open and close.
How to savor the savagery of Egyptians,
Who betrayed the names of their gods
To demons, and tore the hair
From their godheads
As lotus blossoms are pulled out of the pool.

The Prophet Announces

*On an illustration from an
eighteenth-century Haggadah*

And so they arrive for all the world to see,
Elijah with the shofar to his mouth,
His hand upon the guide reins of the King,
Who rides an ass. They look so sad.
In all, a quiet scene, unless the shofar's sound
I barely hear was louder in that century.
Behind them is a tree, and on its branch
A startled bird, to say there's hope of life.
Old images of immortality.
But where's new Adam come to greet the King?
Unless this be the moment of their setting out,
And no one's heard that death's been done and even
Now the first light's traveling from the east.

Exodus

When they escaped
They carried a pack of bones
In a mummy-coffin like an ark.
Of course they had the pillar
Of clouds by day and fire by night,
But those were like dreams
Or something painted on the sky.
God was in the bones
Because Joseph had said
God will remember you
If you take me hence.
This was before the miracle
By the sea or the thundering mountain,
Before the time of thrones
And cherubim. They were
Only now drawn forth
To eat the history feast
And begin the journey.
Why then should they carry history
Like an ark, and the remembering
Already begun?

Aleph

Oxhead, working in
The intelligence. First sign,
Alphabet's wedge.
Followed by house, fish,
Man praying, palm of hand,
Water, serpent,
Eye, and so forth – cross.
Whence to
Hebrew-Phoenician abstract
And so to Greek.
But to return to first
Signs when the world's
Complex –
The head of an ox
Blunt, blundering,
Withal intelligencer
Pushing forward, horns raised,
Stirring the matter
To make a beginning
For Amos, Homer,
And all who came first
In that sign.

A Short History

Urbanity obscures the mystery.
From the fiery limits of His crown
The brawling letters broke,
In the beginning.
Violence on the historical track.
Then distances – prophet, king –
And the voltage that enabled them
To strike their meaning
And to stand. When the palmed word
Issued anodyne. The rest is mockery.

Feast of the Ram's Horn

As seventh sign, the antique heavens show
A pair of scales. And Jews, no less antique,
Hear the ramrod summons beat their heels,
Until they stand together in mock show
As if they meant to recognize a king.

For they are come again to this good turning:
That from the mountain where their leader goes,
In ten days' time they greet the Law descending.
And these are ancient stories from a book
That circulates, and for them has no ending.

All stand as witness to the great event.
Ezra, their scribe, before the water gate
Takes up the book, and the people rise.
And those who weep upon the word are bid
To hold their peace because the day is holy.

Feast of the ram's horn. Let the player rise.
And may the sound of that bent instrument,
In the seventh month, before the seventh gate,
Speak for all the living and the dead,
And tell creation it is memorized.

Let Isaac be remembered in the ram
That when the great horn sounds, and all are come,
These who now are gathered as one man
Shall be gathered again. Set the bright
Scales in the sky until that judgment's done.

Spirit of Rabbi Nachman

'The word moves a bit of air,
And this the next, until it reaches
The man who receives the word of his friend
And receives his soul therein
And is therein awakened' –
Rabbi Nachman's preachment on the word,
Which I gloomily thumb
Wondering how it is with me
That I am not yet on the first
Rung (and many with me!).
To move a bit of air!

If a man ask, can he have
This thing, whether it be
An infusion of soul, or souls,
Steadfast to complete the journeying?
Words moving a bit of air
So that the whole morning moves.

Battle Report

1

The Adriatic was no sailor's sea.
We raced above that water for our lives
Hoping the green curve of Italy
Would take us in. Rank, meaningless fire

That had no other object but our life
Raged in the stunned engine. I acquired
From the scene that flickered like a silent film
New perspective on the days of man.

Now the aviators, primed for flight,
Gave to the blue expanse can after can
Of calibers, armored clothes, all
The rich paraphernalia of our war.

Death in a hungry instant took us in.
He touched me where my lifeblood danced
And said, the cold water is an ample grin
For all your twenty years.

Monotone and flawless, the blue sky
Shows to my watching face this afternoon
The chilled signal of our victory.
Again the lost plane drums home.

2

No violence rode in the glistening chamber.
For the gunner the world was unhinged.
Abstract as a drinker and single
He hunched to his task, the dumb show
Of surgical fighters, while flak, impersonal,
Beat at the floor that he stood on.

The diamond in his eye was fear;
It barely flickered.
From target to target he rode.
The images froze, the flak hardly mattered.
Europe rolled to its murderous knees
Under the sex of guns and cannon.

In an absence of pain he continued,
The oxygen misting his veins like summer.
The bomber's long sleep and the cry of the gunner,
Who knows that the unseen mime in his blood
Will startle to terror,
Years later, when love matters.

3
My pilot dreamed of death before he died.
That stumbling Texas boy
Grew cold before the end, and told
The bombardier, who told us all.
We worried while we slept.
And when he died, on that dark morning
Over Italy in clouds,
We clapped him into dirt.
We counted it for enmity
That he had fraternized with death.
From hand to hand
We passed in wonderment
The quicksilver of our lives.

4
I turn my rubber face to the blue square
Given me to trace the fighters
As they weave their frost, and see
Within this sky the traffic
Fierce and heavy for the day:

All those who stumbling home at dark
Found their names fixed
Beside a numbered Fort, and heard
At dawn the sirens rattling the night away,
And rose to that cold resurrection
And are now gathered over Italy.

In this slow dream's rehearsal,
Again I am the death-instructed kid,
Gun in its cradle, sun at my back,
Cities below me without sound.
That tensed, corrugated hose
Feeding to my face the air of substance,
I face the mirroring past.
We swarm the skies, determined armies,
To seek the war's end, the silence stealing,
The mind grown hesitant as breath.

News of the World

The past, like so many bad poems,
Waits to be reordered,
And the future needs reordering too.
Rain dampens the brick,
And the house sends up its smell
Of smoke and lives –
My own funk the major part.
Angling for direction,
I think of the favored in Homer,
Who in a dream, a council meeting,
At the bottom of despair,
Heard the voice of a god or goddess,
Though it was, say, only Polites
Speaking. Turning to a friend,
I ask again
For news of the world.

Monday

Everybody thinks the past is real.
The window and the skull
Admit light. The past comes through
Like that – undifferentiated,
Hallucinatory, of no weight.
Sleepless that night, he saw the
Room close-woven, a nest
Of chairs, tables, rug
The past was filtering through.
It had no odor, no
Emotion. You could not
Say that in the silences
The past came in
Like water over sand.
There was no movement.
You could not draw the blind.

Past Time

I believe we came together
Out of ignorance not love,
Both being shy and hunted in the city.
In the hot summer, touching each other,
Amazed at how love could come
Like a waterfall, with frightening force
And bruising sleep. Waking at noon,
Touching each other for direction,
Out of ignorance not love.

Sunday Morning

You begin to tell a story.
I perceive it is to be
Another of those unpunctuated excursions
Into the country of my failures.
You, pointing to the familiar landmarks.
I, nodding in assent.
We settle back.

ABC of Culture

So the angel of death whistles Mozart
(As we knew he would)
Bicycling amid the smoke of Auschwitz,
The Jews of Auschwitz,
In the great museum of Western Art.

Purities

What was ceremonially impure, he knew,
Was his life. The laws were not followed.
The god was unhonored.
Anxiety sat on every road.
To change his life, he invented
A job that promised regularity and order.
He invented love that promised joy.
In summer he sat among green trees.
The family laughed in water.
Now let the ceremony begin, he said,
In the heart of summer,

In the pure green
And the pure blue.
Let the god walk his mountain.
He can come down.

Lines for the Ancient Scribes

The past sends images to beach
Upon our present consciousness.
The sons of light war with the sons
Of darkness still. The congregations
Of the sleek and sure rule at will.

Jerome and Origen can tell
How Greek redactions of the text
Stalled at the Tetragrammaton.
And violent in archaic script
The Name burned upon parchment –

Whence springs the ram to mind again
From whose sinews David took
Ten strings to fan upon his harp.
So that the sacrifice was song,
Though ash lay on the altar stone.

The Night

Memory, my own prince of disaster,
My ancient of night.
In the scored silence
I see the dead.
They file past the fixed camera –
The ritual wave, and the smile,
And good night. For an instant
They are there, caught
In their clothes and their gestures;
White faces glow
In the murk of the film,
Absurdly alive. How little I own
This family of the dead,
Who are now part of night.
Memory, my own prince of disaster,
When you go,
Where's the night?

The Six Hundred Thousand Letters

The day like blank paper
Being pulled from my typewriter.
With the six
Hundred thousand letters of the Law
Surrounding me,
Not one of them in place.

National Cold Storage Company

The National Cold Storage Company contains
More things than you can dream of.
Hard by the Brooklyn Bridge it stands
In a litter of freight cars,
Tugs to one side; the other, the traffic
Of the Long Island Expressway.
I myself have dropped into it in seven years
Midnight tossings, plans for escape, the shakes.
Add this to the national total –
Grant's tomb, the Civil War, Arlington,
The young President dead.
Above the warehouse and beneath the stars
The poets creep on the harp of the Bridge.
But see,
They fall into the National Cold Storage Company
One by one. The wind off the river is too cold,
Or the times too rough, or the Bridge
Is not a harp at all. Or maybe
A monstrous birth inside the warehouse
Must be fed by everything – ships, poems,
Stars, all the years of our lives.

For WCW

Now they are trying to make you
The genital thug, leader
Of the new black shirts –
Masculinity over all!
I remember you after the stroke
(Which stroke? I don't remember which stroke.)
Afraid to be left by Flossie
In a hotel lobby, crying out
To her not to leave you
For a minute. Cracked open
And nothing but womanish milk
In the hole. Only a year
Before that we were banging
On the door for a girl to open,
To both of us. Cracked,
Broken. Fear
Slaughtering the brightness
Of your face, stroke and
Counterstroke, repeated and
Repeated, for anyone to see.
And now, grandmotherly,
You stare from the cover
Of your selected poems –
The only face you could compose
In the end. As if having
Written of love better than any poet
Of our time, you stepped over
To that side for peace.
What valleys, William, to retrace
In memory, after the masculine mountains,
What long and splendid valleys.

Days and Nights

1

You keep beating me down.
When I reach a balance,
You break it, always
Clawing for the heart.
In the electric light
We face each other.
Whatever you want of me,
Goddess of insomnia and pure form,
It's not these messages I scratch out
Morning after morning
To turn you off.

2

Whether I had room
For all that joy
In my economy
Is another matter.
Rejecting me,
She shut out all my light,
Showed to me the backs
Of houses, tail lights
Going fast,
Smiles disappearing.
Every man
Was my enemy.
So it was for many a day.
I could not
Climb out of it,
So close was I
To her will.

3

'He that is wise may correct natures.'
Alchemy. The philosophical stone.
Your shadow over the page.
Your hair to my cheek.
Your eyes great riding lights
In the alcoholic storm that now
I remember, along with that
Bruising sweat of rhetoric
I thought appropriate to the times.
He that is wise
May have his life to remember.
But I am reduced to reciting
The letters of the alphabet.
If I say them with fervor
(Saying them with fervor)
Will memory be stirred?
Your own goddess-voice
In the leaves, in the night
Of the body, as I turn the page.

4

Well, it was only Bottom's dream –
Methought I was and
Methought I had.
Outside, the sky is a field
In which the seeds of minerals shine.
And I am hunched over the board
On which I write my nights
Breathing configurations
On the winter air. As far from you
As ever I was far from you.
The cold locks everything in place.
Now I am here. The flame of my match
Everything that is given to me.

5

Suddenly I see your face close up
And all my senses scramble
To get the shock
Home again. In sleep
Not knowing who I am
Or however that spent match struck.

6

The white brilliance under the eyelids
So that all things appear to me
In that color. The worlds you see
Exist in joy. Eyes like doves.
Equilibrium, a white brilliance.

7

Now you come again
Like a very patient ghost,
Offering me Zen records,
A discourse on the stomach
As the seat of the soul,
Your long white neck to kiss.
The tiger's eye that is
Your favorite jewel
Shines in your hand.
Wanting to, I can't conjure
You up, not a touch.
Unbidden, you cross a thousand miles
To say, This is the gift
I was going to give you forever.

The Light Is Sown

The light is sown.
It is there, under the stones
That have been flung
On the street.
Behind my house now
It is in full flower.
The leaves of the mimosa
Are edged with light.
This is the gift
I have and do not claim.
If I could take
The world like that –
All things to which
The light adheres:
Your body edged with light
Which I claim
And count on
And lose
And claim again.

By the Women's House of Detention

Love is the beggar's itch
And I depart
Past the stockaded women, tier on tier,
Singing the same song
Through their delicate home.

Sundays, the colored lesbians
Lean in the street and cry
Up to the latticed windows
Love's old sweet song.

Happy in these streets
I see out of some dark cellar
Orpheus lead Eurydice

While past me goes
Young Icarus, his red heart
Bleating like a sheep
In the fall from perpetual music.

This summer, like a jungle,
I dream in a confusion of chairs
As love over the ancient city
Flares like an angel's eye.

Sister

My dead sister dreams away her life.
About forty years of dreaming
As I count.
My father blamed my mother
For the child's death
And wasn't at the funeral.
The tears, the tears she bred
In me out of my sister's loss,
Weeping of hurt, deprivation, age,
The insanity of life.
My sister, eager for her share,
Under such a tiny headstone
In a city we never pass.
Kin, dreaming dark poems
That spill into my life.

Riverside Drive

from the Yiddish of Joseph Rolnick

Pulling myself out of bed,
I leave the house.
The blueness caresses me.
The wind pushes my hair.
A whole world of quiet
I fill with my steps
On the sidewalk,
And in the street,
The milkman's horse.
Somewhere, on a higher floor,
Along a dark corridor,
The milkman makes his shining rows.
Running, the papers
Under my arm,
I don't look at numbers.
I know the way
Like the horse.
The sun is already up
On the east side of the city.
Its flames, its grace
Spill, whole canfuls, on the cliffs
Of the Jersey shore.
At 310 Riverside Drive
A man on a low balcony,
Young but with mustache and beard –
His appearance not of here –
Stretches a hand toward
The west and shouts
Something like, See there!
And I stand like him
With my papers raised
Like an offering
To the light.
The two of us
Come for the first time

To this place,
To the red cliffs
Of this morning.

Ditty

Where did the Jewish god go?
Up the chimney flues.
Who saw him go?
Six million souls.
How did he go?
All so still
As dew from the grass.

Where I Am Now

Every morning I look
Into the world
And there is no renewal.
Every night, my lids clamped,
I concentrate
On the renewal to come.

I am on the lookout for
A great illumining,
Prepared to recognize it
Instantly and put it to use
Even among the desks
And chairs of the office, should
It come between nine and five.

A Message from Rabbi Nachman

The extra-human
Swarms with disciples.
Like worms
Tumbling out of the Book of Creation,
The Book of Splendor.
Each with a light
In his head.
But smeared with
The contemplation of ecstasy.

Kabbalah –
A transmission
From mouth to ear.
The words of my friend
Steady my world
Even as I say them.

There are stones –
How else will the house
Be built –
Like souls
That are flung down
In the streets.

Lines for Erwin R. Goodenough (1893-1965)

'If Aphrodite could take Moses
From the ark in the Nile
In the synagogue at Dura'

Naked as she was
Her breasts blue-pointed

If Aphrodite could move
Among these sheols
Of the dead

If she to ornament the dark
Could bend her body
To the water
Promising life
From the mother

'Come down upon this cup which stands before me,
Fill it with grace and a holy spirit,
So that it becomes for me a new plant within me.'

Cross Country

The night's traffic.
I can barely follow the markers,
My eyes stung with seeing.
Snow in the mountains
Is so beautiful.
All through the chemical wastes
Of New Jersey
I follow my guide –
Rare truths in the mountains –
While the kids
Sleep in the back with my wife.
No one to see me
For the dazzling snow.

For Delmore Schwartz

1
How do they go on living?
How does anyone go on living?
A woman kills her three children
In 1954. In 1966 she kills
Another three. And the husband
Continues to go to work
At the same job. Which
Is to be judged insane?
And we keep walking the same
Roads, past mayhem, slaughter
Of innocents – this morning, the granny
Curled up beside her bottle
Of Petri wine at a side door
Of the Paramount – every day,
Leading sensible lives.
The sirens seem never to stop,
Even in the country, amid
Crickets or ocean sound.
What we all know,
What keeps humming in the back
Of the brain. When the language
Pauses, the killing begins.

2
  our intelligence was so clear
In your first poems, like
Mozart in his music.
Yet it could not help you,
As you said,
When the old arguments,
The din around the family table,
Grew louder all about you –
The arguments we endlessly rehearse
When mind loses its own motion.

Then our jaws lock into the face
We had, on the words we said
Under our breath, to ourselves,
To our underselves, so fiercely deep
They were for years beyond hearing,
And now do all the talking.

3
Disturbed by dreams,
I wake into the chilled morning.
The dreams are rich
With patterns of rejection
(Mother, Wife), suicide and loss.
A victim of such disasters,
When I awake I judge myself
Harshly and long.
Four A.M. on a vacation morning.
The surf takes over in my head, a running
Commentary, a Greek chorus,
Saying something like, nothing but the sea.
In my universe of feeling,
I can hear the sea. These dreams,
Bits of genre, Viennese pastry,
From which I awake, stuffed
With bourgeois living, these dreams
Of the dead fathers I believe in . . .

From Martin Buber

'A story must be told in such a way
That it constitutes help in itself.'
Or not the way telephone addicts
Trap themselves for eternity
In a recital of symptoms –
Blood pressure, urine, sleep –
Saying tonight what they will
Relive tomorrow.

(Finding you whole
After a night of hatred
World to my touch
Like bread to my touch
Which I ceaselessly crumble
And the loaf is there.)

(Or when the traffic slurs
Early in the morning
Of a long night
And I strike it rich
With calm.)

Through the Boroughs

I hear the music from the street
Every night. Sequestered at my desk,
My luminous hand finding the dark words.
Hard, very hard. And the music
From car radios is so effortless.
And so I strive to join my music
To that music. So that
The air will carry my voice down
The block, across the bridge,
Through the boroughs where people I love
Can hear my voice, saying to them
Through the music that their lives
Are speaking to them now, as mine to me.

Notes at 46

What distinguishes our work
Is an American desperation.
Who thought to find this
In the new world?

I owe my father a tribute.
On his last day
When the head nurse
Asked what he wanted
He said, I want to
Look into the eyes of a young girl.

The eyes of a young girl.
I want to look into
The eyes of a young girl.

It's nothing to me
Who gathers us in.
And it's nothing to me
Who owns us now.

I can think of Venice
Or Jerusalem.
Armand's little goat beard
Quivers in the spring.

It suddenly strikes me
That at forty-six
I want to write the lyrics
Of a boy of twenty
So I blow my brains out.

Not wanting to invent emotion
I pursued the flat literal,
Saying wife, children, job
Over and over.
When the words took on
Emotion I changed their order.
In this way, I reached daylight
About midnight.

'I wish I had never been born!'
He shouts at six.
A pure despair.
At forty-six I cannot say that
With honesty.
Pure passion is beyond me.
Everything is mixed.
Grief allied with joy –
That he is able to say it!

In October the house is chill.
Still, the cricket of summer
Sings, reminding us of promises.
As long as the heart listens
It pumps blood.

Riding Westward

It's holiday night
And crazy Jews are on the road,
Finished with fasting and high on prayer.
On either side of the Long Island Expressway
The lights go spinning
Like the twin ends of my tallis.
I hope I can make it to Utopia Parkway
Where my father lies at the end of his road.
And then home to Brooklyn.
Jews, departure from the law
Is equivalent to death.
Shades, we greet each other.
Darkly, on the Long Island Expressway,
Where I say my own prayers for the dead,
Crowded in Queens, remembered in Queens,
As far away as Brooklyn. Cemeteries
Break against the City like seas,
A white froth of tombstones
Or like schools of herring, still desperate
To escape the angel of death.
Entering the City, you have to say
Memorial prayers as he slides overhead
Looking something like my father approaching
The Ark as the gates close on the Day of Atonement
Here in the car and in Queens and in Brooklyn.

Saul's Progress

1
I told my son:
'Stop trying the screw the monkey's tail
Into his bellybutton.
Originality
Is never its own
Justification.
Some innovations
Get nowhere.'

'The Sunday monkeys are my friends,'
He said.
I was on my way down
From the heavenly city
Of the 18th Century philosophers.
He was on his way up,
Almost three.

2
'Moby Dick is smarter than
The other dicks.'
A song to make the
Bad guys happy.
You sang it all day Saturday
With snot-filled nose
And clouded eye,
To raise me
To a fury.

3

You sit on the crest of a dune
Facing the sea,
Which is beyond sight.
Your anger at me
Makes you play by yourself,
Tell stories to yourself,
Fling out your hurt
To the wide sky's healing.
A red boat in one hand,
A blue in the other,
You begin singing songs
About the weather.
Cliff swallow, brilliant skimmer.

4

As if he were me, he comes bounding in,
All happiness. I owe him
All happiness. For these years at least.
When he smiles and says, a good time,
I have no notion who else
He has made happy with my happiness.

Veteran

1

I never thought I'd be a survivor
And base everything on that strategy.
Closing in on fifty, almost un-American,
Out of it, I'm close to myself again
In my fifty-mission photo –
Poised in leather jacket, parachute harness,
By the twin guns of the bomber –
Breathing now,
Twenty, numb, a survivor.

2

To open myself to the wars,
The TV newsreels,
The savage fighting.
To walk with this knowledge,
To see light in this light.
Which was my own youngness.
The shell exploding under the fuselage.
Smoke drifting through the cabin.
Hearing the shell, smelling the smoke.
Knowing it is fire. Making that knowledge
Be with me in the everyday.
Opening my eyes to the sunlight,
Frozen, the condition of my will.
Looking through that to my childhood,
My children.

3
Frozen and baffled,
There is nothing
To be gained
From searching that time.
If one had an answer –
How use it?
Instead, there is the victory
Of being here
With what one has
Like the world itself
That lives
Through time.

A Gift

She made him a gift of her touch,
Softly turning the collar of his jacket down
In the crowded elevator. To say,
See, my spirit still hovers to protect.
That he could prize such useless moments.

Motorbikes break the night's silence.
The President's face on the television screen.
Green on my set. Words muffling perception.
Everything keeps us from the truth, which
Begins to have a religious presence.
Why so many claim it, in the tail of the tiger
Or elsewhere. No matter. When I find it,
Being so rare, it is fiercer than whiskey.
My eyes burn with happiness and I speak
Collected into myself.

Like a Beach

Even the unlived life within us
Is worth examining.
Maybe it is all we have.
The rest is burned up
Like fuel in the furnace.
But the unlived life
Stretches within us like a beach.
There is a gull's shadow on it.
Or it is at night and the moon
Crusts the sand.
Or it is a house at night
With people talking in the next room
Over cards.
                    You believe
In these observations?
Doesn't the sea sweep in,
The action begin in the house
At night, the voices of the players
Loud in argument,
Their motives, their needs,
Turbulent as the sea?
Whose happiness
Even here
Is being sacrificed?

Muse Poem

While I'm waiting for the words,
Could you just
Lean over me a little,
That way,
With your breasts
Of imagination, incense,
And blue dawns.

It is always the same quiet night.
You in your desperation say,
'What you are writing is poetry.
No one will read it.'
You worry about my health
When I find I am not
To be famous. But I am
Already inside you in my thoughts.

City Portrait

Her husband didn't give her highs,
Just made her lows less low.
Said, with the lips trembling.
Breasts too, I think.
Beautiful woman.
Going to bed with strangers now.
Trying to think it all out.
On the west side of Manhattan,
Twelve floors above the murderous streets.

47th Street

In the delicatessen
The countermen
Were bantering about the Messiah,
Lifting the mounds of corned beef
And tongue. He wouldn't come,
They said, you couldn't
Count on it. Meaning:
They would die in harness.

Cry of Small Rabbits

The cry of the small rabbits facing death.
Nobody would want to sing like that.
A short, high wailing. So what
If death gave them voice to sing?
I face my own rage and fear, tearing for words
That I can say calmly in sentences
That will not stop. I want to see
The next line glitter, and the last
Come crashing like surf.

August

Ancient mariner, your gray beard
Dries in the sun, salt sparkling
The wires. Beached on this vacation coast,
You have forgotten your story.
It's drifted away among children,
Scrub pine, the chattering sea.
And there is no one to hold
By the eye or sweet tit anyway.
Better to whistle with the birds
And pick berries in the sun.

Domestic Matters

1
It wasn't what I had thought –
Children taking up
Most of the house, leaving
Me (or so it often seems)
Only room enough
For the bed. Which itself
Is a kind of relic, as if
From an earlier
Marriage. And so you turn
In the bedroom door,
White, and so small,
To say good night.
To say there are
Two of us.

2

I am crying over this body of yours
Which is to wither in the dust.
Already your belly's thrust outpoints
Your breasts. The hair of your head
Grows thin. A skeleton
Smiles to me with your gums.

3

We are almost
Out of earshot
Of one another
Yet our answers
Seem to find
Connected questions
Of an urgency
So deep, they might
Be coming
From the center
Of a life.

4

We were comrades
In a disastrous war.
We have created a history
That will be sung
In the psyche of others.
Troy's burning
And the flames may light us
All the way to death.

O Seasons

1

It seemed reasonable to expect an answer.
That was an early feeling, like owning something.
Urban dawn, and yet to hear the birds.
I must have that happiness.

2

Speculations about man's soul:
A face within a face,
The transformer, the perfecting agent
In the disassembled gear I carry
With me into day. Crossing the street
Steam flurries from the underground.
My life as hidden as the godhead
On 43rd and Broadway where garments
Of light wrap the tall buildings
And I step forth, fierce to know.

3

Excuse this boy from life
I wanted my mother to write
As I went off to school.
It would take a cosmic jubilee
To make my soul ascend
From this despair. If I could say
My native home, and turn
In that direction, glass in hand,
Crossing the crowded room
As once I came to you.
These misinformed meditations
Hurrying the world's
Return to waste and void.

4

So I come home
And the cherub next door
Is singing Hawaiian songs
In a contralto. His job
Must be as tough as mine.

5

It's true I was timid
On my way to Esau in the Sixties.
Someone said, 'The place to which we are going
Is not subject to any law,
Because all that is on the side of death;
But we are going to life.' It was
Her heart-shaped ass made me do it.
Descriptions of wreckage. The blown windows
Of a town house in Manhattan.
Fucking in the desert.

6

Wind in the leaves along the street.
Another year is hurried to its close.
Today I passed a man struck down
On 33rd street. Yesterday,
On the steps of the Borough Hall station
I saw another gone, eyes open
To the sifting, grayish light.

7

Bordering on vacancy at the year's end.
The whole continent unpeopled.
The created uncreate. The monuments
Crawled back into cold stone. The thick husks.
One thousand nine hundred and seventy-seven
Years of christendom, dumb in this believer,
Cherishing the light to come on the bleak
Cityscape – vacant lot on the street
To Jehovah's Kingdom, by the peerless bridge.

A Notebook

At the bare edge
The images seem fabulous.

I certainly didn't
Wear myself out
With brilliance,

'It is forbidden to be old' (Nachman).

If you steam-blast the bricks
In Brooklyn, they will
Come up bright as Henry James.

Dead Indians are in the underbrush
Waiting for the word.

I don't like you
And I don't know
Anyone else.

The stars be hid
That led me to this pain.

I stroke my wife's angel hair
Thinking of you.

It is a bowl of blue light.
It will be there all day
Now that I have seen it.

I take out my old anxieties
And they still work.

A notebook of dry cunts.

Why is everything discussed
With that high cackle?
Ladies, I weep for beauty
And you bear it.

I used to visit bombed-out towns.
Now I visit bombed-out people.
There's a kind of beautiful smell
To both, which I can't
Put out of my mind.

Man, the master of choice.

Words, rushing into judgment.

All right, you mother stickers,
This is a fuck up.

Musical Shuttle

Night, expositor of love.
Seeing the sky for the first time
That year, I watched the summer constellations
Hang in air: Scorpio with
Half of heaven in his tail.
Breath, tissue of air, cat's cradle.
I walked the shore
Where cold rocks mourned in water
Like the planets lost in air.
Ocean was a low sound.
The gatekeeper suddenly gone,
Whatever the heart cried
Voice tied to dark sound.
The shuttle went way back then,
Hooking me up to the first song
That ever chimed in my head.
Under a sky gone slick with stars,
The aria tumbling forth:
Bird and star.
However those cadences
Rocked me in the learning years,
However that soft death sang –
Of star become a bird's pulse,
Of the spanned distances
Where the bird's breath eddied forth –
I recovered the lost ground.
The bird's throat
Bare as the sand on which I walked.
Love in his season
Had moved me with that song.

The Realization

If one could follow a man
Through the places of his exile,
Asking him at each point
Why he had strayed from his life
Or been turned from it,
In time the dialogue
Would be meaningless
For the exile would be the life.
So we live.

Lines

Blue darkening. A bar of it.
Dan calls to say he'll be home by ten;
Do I mind if he's out that late.
I smoke a cigar, study the page,
Cherish the silence. My paint-
Smeared pants pronounce me
The captain of good works.
Happy homesteader, husband.
So I never trafficked in guns
In Africa. And I became myself
And not another. My own vacillations
Rampant in my lines.
Responsibility on my abraded shoulders.
Singer of neurasthenia, or something like it,
Was my aim. What wings touch
Me now out of the darkening blue?

Things Seen

There is no natural scenery like this:
when her loose gown from her shoulders
falls, the light hardens, shadows
move slowly, my breath catches.

The flame of the blue cornflower,
a half inch above the flower,
fanned by wind.

July

You poets of the Late T'ang send me messages
    this morning.
The eastern sky is streaked with red.
Linkages of bird song make a floating chain.
In a corner of the world, walled in by ocean
    and sky,
I can look back on so many destructive days
    and nights,
and forward too, ego demons as far as
    mind reaches.
Here, for a moment, the light holds.

May 14, 1978

The poet Kenji Miyazawa asks me,
What world is it you want to enter?
Percussive rain on the early morning window.
The house, the steady breathing, focused now
on the lighted surface of my desk.
I cannot answer him for joy and dread.

City

Silver dawn over Madison Avenue.
The refrigerator shuts softly, like a kiss.

He is dying of the terminal cutesies
she says of the cultural journalist,
the newspaper spread before her on the table.
Thousands fail in her sight daily.

The word 'happiness'
like the sun in late March
is a light I can see
but not feel. There it is
on the back of my hand
as real as my hand
clenched now
against the wind on 48th Street.

In Great Neck, at 4:30 in the morning,
Ring Lardner and Scott Fitzgerald
walk the streets. American success
is their theme. The sleepers drink it in
across the lawns.

In the lamp's circle,
warmed by bourbon,
I play the role out. It is
not to tell the world
anything. What is it
the world would want to know?

Her furious body, plunged into sleep.
On the pillow, her live hair,
helmet and cloak. What I say in the room
is for me and the walls. We are doing darkness,
each in his own way.

The Wish

This night in Brooklyn is as ancient
as nights get, though the moon
hangs like a lamp, and the traffic
slurs in my room.
My desire is as sharp as whiskey
or a hurt nerve, from my head
to my hand: to populate
the void, to turn this blankness
into a field of stars, where I can sleep
forever in my earned sleep,
comforted by the wind off Atlantic
Avenue, and the waters at its end.
Lights rise from the water, a City
across the way, that I raise
in my empty room to starlight.

Learning

1

He is back in a student's room
having learned nothing
in 35 years, except
despair and happiness are sweeter
to him now, they are purer
to his taste, as if he had
learned to discriminate among
his emotions, to say this is
despair and this is happiness.

2

Paying dues –
you imagine this is
a creative loneliness.
You are aware of wind
or traffic rushing in
the street. You think
God is as lost as you:
'the fixed points vanished,
the beginning and the end
both forgotten. Day
after day the light
is its own explanation.

3

In my room a bug climbs the white wall
or rather seems to be thinking of climbing it.
I too would like to get to the top of something.

4
Rabbi Nachman's final message:
Gevalt! Do not despair!
There is no such thing as despair at all!
Shouted from the very depths of the heart.

On a Sunday

When you write something
you want it to live –
you have that obligation, to give it
a start in life.
Virginia Woolf, pockets full of stones,
sinks into the sad river
that surrounds us daily. Everything
about London amazed her, the shapes
and sights, the conversations on a bus.
At the end of her life, she said,
London is my patriotism.
I feel that about New York.
Would Frank O'Hara say, Virginia Woolf,
get up? No, but images from her novels
stay in my head – the old poet,
Swinburne, I suppose, sits on the lawn
of the country house, mumbling
into the sun. Pleased with the images,
I won't let the chaos of my life
overwhelm me. There is the City,
and the sun blazes on Central Park
in September. These people, on a Sunday,
are beautiful, various. And the poor
among them make me think
the experience I knew will be relived again,
so that my sentences will keep hold
of reality, for a while at least.

Brooklyn Heights

1

I'm on Water Street in Brooklyn,
between the Brooklyn Bridge
and the Manhattan Bridge,
the high charge of their traffic
filling the empty street.
Abandoned warehouses
on either side.
In the shadowed doorways, shades
of Melville and Murder Incorporated.
Five o'clock October light.
Jets and gulls in the fleecy sky.
Climbing the hill to Columbia Heights,
I turn to see the cordage
of the Brooklyn Bridge, and behind it
the battle-gray Manhattan.

2

This room shelved high with books
echoes with my midnights. Pages
of useless lines swim in it. Only
now and then a voice cuts through
saying something right: No sound
is dissonant which tells of life.
The gaudy ensigns of this life
flash in the streets; a December light,
whipped by wind, is at the windows.
Even now the English poets are in the street,
Keats and Coleridge on Hicks Street,
heading for the Bridge. Swayed aloft there,
the lower bay before them, they can
bring me back my City line by line.

Cummings

On May nights, in Patchin Place,
Greenwich Village of my memory,
girls from Smith and Vassar
vagabonding for the weekend,
lovely in the alley light,
would chant up to the shy poet's
window: How do you like your blue-
eyed boy, Mr Death. And indeed
Buffalo Bill's defunct – pencil-thin
by the alley gate, sketchbook in hand,
open collar of the artist, across
from the Women's House of Detention
in the waning light of afternoons.

Blue Eyes

Young women with the baby fat
still on them, smelling of milk.
Against that, her bravery –
striding out of bed in the morning,
her years, her children underfoot,
her blue eyes flashing warning.

'I could make some of these guys very happy,'
she said, looking up from the personals
in the *New York Review of Books*.

You read to her of war,
devastation, gut-chilling
insecurity, and her blue eyes
waver, and she sleeps
like an American child.

'Is this a peak experience?'
she said, sliding down beside him,
her blue eyes laughing at his desperate age.

Sound of surf through dense fog.
Moisture streaming from the screened windows.
'Where are the beautiful love poems?'
she keeps asking him.

She became the line
he had in his head
just before sleep, that
he thought he would retain
and now it's gone.

The End

Imagine your own death.
I'm wearing my father's
gray tweed overcoat.
I've just had a corned beef
sandwich on 47th Street

(I asked for lean
and it came fat,
I should have sent it
back) when it hits me
in the chest.

A Memorial

My mother and father on the town,
in the photograph. American jazz
in the swing of her handbag
banging from her wrist.
Spats, and the woman
with a white rose in her hair.
Hey, this was
a big romance. He was making money,
going to make more money. Everything
was looking up.
I love them in this photograph.

Saturday

It is noon and you don't know
what to do with your life.
It always begins again,
so you wait for it to begin again.
Then come the songs, then comes
the bitterness, then comes
the glorious end.

It was a rhythmic vitality
in her laugh, her walk.
What else was I to do?
The way her eyes widen
is still with me. Shall I forget
the mystery of women because
I sleep alone?

Waking unhappy and alone
at two A.M. is the way
you wanted to be. You can
put on the light.
There's no one to disturb.
That taste in your mouth
is your dream:
infidelity, cowardice, fear.
The way God wanted me to be,
I cry, opening me up,
feeling through the soft entrails
for a few hard grains of truth.

A heroic deception, learned
from Levine (for whom it may
be true), but as for you, you
like the gloom and the taste
in your mouth, you choose it
and you call it life.

Battlements

for H.R. Hays

These dark colors I place against
the blue heron at Louse Point. Summer
eternal, though after we go,
it may all be paved over.

Into the calm morning
steps the blue heron. The shore
oscillates like a nest to his leaving.

The old poet is brought down to look at the bay.
He thinks he has never done justice to anything
    in his poems.
Gulls crack shells on the macadam road.
Returning, held by others, he urinates by the car.

When you die, who will come out
to meet you if not the blue heron.

A Jerusalem Notebook

1
A city of ascensions,
nowhere to go but up.
Forcing the spirit in New York
is the commonplace; we live
there as if we were in Jerusalem,
Jesus and Mohammed touching down
and going up, just another
launching pad, as I get off
the bus and head home.

2 *Postcard*
It is not far from here
that the parents stood
and the child, placed into the priest's machine,
heard the wail
of Moloch. And the bronze god,
arms outstretched, smiled at the smoke.
Two of the kings of Judah
burned their sons here –
Hell, Gehenna, Gai Hinnom,
the pleasant valley of Hinnom,
pink, scarred and silent
in the fading light.

3 *Tourists*

She is crying over three olives
that I threw out. Three olives
but my food, she cries. She is
not a child but a woman.
Outside Zion Gate, Jaffa Gate,
Dung Gate, she rubs my arm slowly.
Gates excite her. Where I come in
at night, the city is so beautiful.

4

It is the temple mount.
It is a little like the temple mount,
though I myself constitute
the sightseers, worshippers,
and sometimes the visiting god.

5

Whatever brought me here, to a new moon
over Zion's hill, dark moon
with the thin cusp silvered,
help me believe in my happiness, for
it was guilt that woke me. A voice
on the telephone crying breakdown.
Illusions of my own ego causing destruction
while outside the marvelous
machinery of day has opened, light
traffic on the road to the citadel.
And as I look again, it is all
swept clean, except for
a faint pink in the sky and on the old
stones of the city, and language in my head
that I brought with me, that I carry,
that I use to mark my way.

6
My way of being in the world:
not perfect freedom or the pitch
of madness, but that the particulars
of my life become manifest
to me walking these dark streets.

7 *For C.R.*
When I dropped permanence from my back
and saw what I had taken for
solid buildings and good roads
was desert all about me and within me,
how bright became the sunlight,
how sweet the evening air.

8 *The Old Jewish Poet Floats in the Dead Sea*
It is the lowest place on earth
but he has been lower.
For example, he has been on the heights
of Masada, watching the Roman soldiers
jack off in the baths below.
He knows his turn will be next.
Beneath him floats a crow.
Beneath the crow floats the crow's shadow.
Beneath the crow's shadow is another Jew.
These Judean junk hills
fill his head with sulphur.
Every hill is a hill of skulls.

9

I understand we are like smoke.
It streams from my cigar into the morning air,
silken, prismlike in sunlight
as I sit by the window.
Nothing I do with my life
could be as beautiful.

10

Lizard lines in his skin.
Striving to become one with the stones
like the lizard, even as the pen
darts into the shadow of the page.

11

I have dreams coming out of my ears,
she said. Why not? This city has seen
so many mad dreamers, their stale dreams
even now looking for new homes.
The stones dream in the sun,
the lizards. In the golden mosque,
riots of line and color, shapes dream
in the marble columns, pulsing in
and out of sleep. When the city wakes
the action is brief and bloody.
Let it sleep. Let the gaberdined Jews
dream of the Messiah. He approaches
the blocked-off gate of the walled city.
Taste the dream of the Jews.

12

Why did I want to sit out all the time,
was the air so special? Yes,
soft and today, dust-blue. But the smell
of corpses had been everywhere, and more to come.
Red buses and blue buses raced the roads
to the small towns, carrying infant Jesuses,
dynamite. Blondes from Scandinavia,
silver-toed, tried on Arab dresses
while the man in the stall scratched his crotch.
It was all happening inside the city.
And at the edge was desert.

13

Middle East music on the radio: Hebrew love songs,
Arab wails. Carmel Dry Gin
taking me up Zion's hill.

14

Who needs more happiness? People living
on the edge (of pain, of death,
of revelation) need time in the sun,
a lengthening interval between
the sonic boom and the rattled glass.

15

I cannot dissever my happiness from language
or from your body. Light a candle for me
at the false tomb of David, I am of that line.
Let the young scarecrow who might be from 47th Street
say a blessing for me. Sway over the candle's flame
like the old Arab riding toward me on his donkey.
If I forget my happiness, let me be dust.
Jerusalem, here I am going up again.
It is your moon, your labyrinths, your desert
crowding east where the sun waits.

Two Cornell Deaths

Because I live I must search these graves.
Coming out of Patchin Place onto 10th Street,
past the iron gate, the figure of Cummings
slouching there, the women ranged
along the street, heads craned
to the barred windows, now silent,
of the Women's House of Detention,
I go to have a drink with Charlie Weir.

He was writing mysteries, working on a novel,
toiling in the wardrobe room of NBC.
In Ithaca he had sometimes missed his classes.
When the train rounded the bend,
hurrying to New York, he flung
his blue books on the tracks, then
marked the grades. For which he was sacked.
Reputed to be a brilliant teacher.

The facts mean nothing in the light of day.
What was the caliber of the weapon?
Partying in Ithaca, thin Jack Sessions
in the corner, another ghost.
He wrote the story of a blind man
who recovered his sight and found
his wife impossibly ugly. She
whom he had loved. What was
the caliber of his weapon, and what other
damage did he do? Last spotted
in a restaurant in the Village.

Pain leaks into this December light.
I take these ghosts with me wherever I go,
asking them, why now? Why this moment?
Because the liquor is inexhaustible,
the girls will stand at the bar
and smile at the stories, as they used to do.
If you walk by the river, Manhattan

is like a book, the pages turn,
the words march down those pages.
Look back to the lights along the river.
Wait for the dark, wait for the city to come on,
windows and bridges blazing.
Whatever you needed was there, wasn't it?

Cynthia

When I take off your red sweatpants,
sliding them over the ass I love,
the fat thighs, and now my hands
are trembling, my tongue is muzzy,
a fire runs under my skin.

Cynthia's red-gold muff caught
the morning light as she strode from my bed,
upright and proud. Her body was
a vehicle for pleasure. It had carried us
into sleep as if we were children,
protected forever from the void and dark.

She slept with him
if at dinner he pleased
her. If he did not, she
did not. She was free
to choose, without
the drags of love.

Every day I wonder about you –
why it is your eyes look so wild
sometimes. Other times, so naked,
so pure-blue naked. Your shields, you say,
speaking of your diaphragm, your contact lenses.
Nevertheless, you think of yourself as being at home

in this world in a way I am not.
I understand it is my myth-making intelligence
gets me in trouble, makes me want to fix you
as earth nourisher, source of comfort,
when it is what is lost and erratic in you
brings you to my bed, beatings against fate
or circumstance, stabbings toward transcendence
that leave us both bruised and happy in ourselves.

To be with her
was to be in a cloud
of sexual joy – hair, eyes,
speech. The merest
flick of her tongue
on a word set off
resonances.

I fell in love with
one of the poisonous tomatoes of America.

Mind-fucking at 3 A.M.
because where are you
and that's where you are.

At the instant of her coming, she makes a throaty sound.
It is back beyond words, low in the throat,
away from the tongue. I never try to translate it,
any more than I would translate sunlight or deep shade.

Before sleep, C in my arms, her back toward me,
puts my right hand on her left breast. If I
could make an amulet of that.

She is beautiful to me
as she wakes from sleep,
sits straight up –
force, energy, and purpose
in her straight spine.

I wonder where her cunt is tonight
and her proud head. She did
make me happy, more than once.
One Sunday morning, light everywhere
in the living room, she on the couch
facing me, garbed in my blue bathrobe,
one breast shapely through the opening
of the robe while I drink my coffee, happy.

The last time
I went down on Cynthia
was the last time though her petals
in the rose red light

　　　She said she had taken on seven students the previous
night on her visit upstate, and that all had watched,
masturbating as each colleague performed. One had her
in the missionary position, one took her from behind,
one made her ride on top, one came in her mouth, one
had her lean over a table, one did her on his lap, one fucked
her up the ass. The last to have her, she said, because
he had come six times, had trouble achieving an erection.
After she had told all this to her lover, fiction or fact,
he became the eighth man.

All the questions she asked him
he answered from another life.

He was trying to understand
the nature of the pain.
Maybe when a woman
aborts a child
it is like this: killing
something in oneself.
Someone else has already done
the killing, yet there
is more left to kill.

She was hidden in his thought
like a tick in a dog's fur.
He could feel the rise with his finger
where her mouth sucked blood.

These Are the Streets

1

The upper strand of the Manhattan Bridge
seen from my window
at five of a December evening –
the lights in a graceful arc,
the lit traffic shuttling the Bridge –
is a piece of God's handiwork now
along with the zebra and the bear.

2

I was part of the restless crowd
but sometimes a hand reached
down for me, pulling me up
into rigor, clarity, real space.

3

Remember when the painters were all doing archaic
        idols?
Things seemed smaller then.
Even mystery was more manageable.
Now it blunders hugely into our lives
like a canvas by Anselm Kiefer.
These are the streets of New York, hung
with letters of white fire on black fire.

Celebrations

The tremendous
cornices of evening.
Freed from work
with the populace
streaming into subways.
Emerging on Court Street.
Turner's sky, his clouds.
To be lifted out of myself.
Mind's eye, cast down,
now lifted up.
Sound carrying the sense
into its own dark home,
furnished with the gold-plated gods
of Egypt, gathering light,
a shadow sliding on sand,
a bird wheeling in the wastes of sky.
Causeless celebrations.
Terns skipping along the surface
beyond the first line of breakers.
And sometimes in the scatter shine
a ripple of bait fish.
The silk twist
of what you said to me.
Zukofsky at the end of the street
under the light, white spats,
derby and a big cigar.
The gang on Delancey Street –
Irving Berlin and my Uncle Abe
trying out tunes.

Questions

The idiot sound of someone's stereo
in the apartment below. The bass thudding
like something caught in a trap.
People live in that racket the way I live
with my questions, the things I don't know.
For example, an image of the successful life,
or what is the good, or how can I get
from here to where I want to be, and where is that.

New York Summer

On my block, on an August night,
the air conditioners whir
like wings trying to take off.
The whole city wants to escape this summer darkness,
to head into an Arctic dawn,
cold and clear, to become an impenetrable
ice city, Leningrad in winter
by the banks of the frozen Neva,
the Puerto Ricans covered in fur,
urging their dogs to drink the mineral-clear
vodka, so the soul can make it
through one more jungle day.

Meditation on a Brooklyn Bench

I was by myself on the promenade,
facing the massive city. Pleasure craft
cut white trails in the water.
The lady with the lamp dim green
in the dim green afternoon.
A Circle Line boat, looking sprightly,
hurrying up river, toward the Bridge,
and the old paddle steamer from
the South Street Seaport meandering
past Battery. The kind of day you
needn't take responsibility for, sitting
in the shade, like an elderly citizen,
wondering where it all went – the wife
and kids, the years of work. Covered over
by the waters of the East River. Not a river,
a tidal basin, and the tide coming in now,
full force, dangerous, looking for me.

Lower East Side

On Houston Street, walking west,
the moon coming up over Katz's Delicatessen,
we pass a synagogue ancient as Tiberias.
You don't have to be touched
by the hand of God
to pick up on these New York clichés.
We get finished walking the dog
and climb to your Catholic-kitsch apartment
where your Mother of God helps me out of my clothes
and history and the ruined smell of these lives.

Years Ago

Rain is in the air, or
falling so gently
it seems part of the air.
My son glides in, leans
his bike beside the porch,
waiting it out. He objects
to my singing 'April Showers'
when it's almost August.
I stop singing
and we listen to the quiet.
When the rain stops
he moves off into the sand
beside the house
to build something with a long
story attached, which he tells
himself as he goes along,
handful by handful.

Lessons

1
At Park Place you make out
what the subway conductor is saying
over the crackling speaker:
'This train is going to the Bronx.'
Then you understand the world extends
beyond your concerns.
You're getting off at 42nd
but this train is going to the Bronx.

2

That gull on the rocks of the East River,
near the pilings of the Brooklyn Bridge,
has the plastic rim of an empty six-pack
around his neck, his beak just
free enough to pick flotsam
from the water. He seems unconcerned,
adjusted, like the rest of us.

3

The man asked me
for some change for a hot meal.
I walked on, hardening my heart
against myself and against my children
and the whole future of the race.

Lit Crit

Street Scene

You are crossing Broadway at 42nd
and you come upon Dante and Virgil
sightseeing, exchanging observations
on the people and the action
as they do in the great poem.
It is winter, and steam from underground
obscures the street. Dante has Virgil
by the arm. You never think
of Dante as a city poet,
but he clearly knows the way.

Crazy Jane Does Yeats

Old he was, limp he was,
I nursed him slowly,
hand and tongue. My finger
in his bunghole. He said,
'Better than Byzantium.'

Poe

Entering Poe's
region of novelty and wonder,
where living inhumation
is the order of the day,
I try to escape the drag
of being the subject of this sentence
dutifully following
the participial phrase
when in fact I am not.
Poe is. It is his America
these days, particularly on the screen.
Arthur Gordon Pym,
lost in Antarctica,
the exhalations of his breath
our starry flag.

Composing

The mind falling through space,
looking for a handhold, a foothold.

Country

Crow's insistence that he knows the way.
Possibly he does. Others have said the same:
Satisfy hunger, for whatever, before night.

Romantics

Thinking about why Byron didn't teach Shelley
to swim that summer in Switzerland,
I see why my fellow feeling
for poets goes just so far.

Library

Cynthia got herself off in the stacks
at UCSD. This thought warms me
as I sit by myself in the library at Duke,
remembering her voice and her careful diction
describe how the desire to manipulate
her clit came from the heavy breathing of lit.

Different Schools

In his arena, travesties.
In mine, a death struggle
(I like to think)
with a hallucinatory beast.
A scorched landscape
across which the hero
comes bearing in his hand
the severed head,
still smoking, eyes red,

emitting words that seem
to contain a promise of sleep.
Meanwhile in his arena,
flags, trumpets, cross-dressing,
and a sun god who looks
like the sun.

Bible Lesson

When it's time for the Sacrifice
Abraham pays for his stardom
with terror and sweat.
The risk of talking with God.
At some point he could say to you:
Listen, this is what I want you to do
for me next, take your son, your only
son whom you love . . .

For Paul Celan and Primo Levi

Because the smoke
still drifted through your lives,
because it had not settled –
what would that settling be?
A coming to terms with man's savagery?
God's savagery? The victim
digging deeper into his wound
for the ultimate face?
That would be like saying
we mourn you, when you
have taken all the mourning words

and left us a gesture
of despair. To understand despair
and be comfortable with it –
something you could not do –
is how we live. Sun
drifting through smoke
as I sit on my roof in Brooklyn
with words for the Days of Awe.

Loyalty

They have been driven insane by history,
my tribe.
They are totally crazy.
Bialik's little Talmudist
and the settler with the gun.
Don't I know firsthand
their self-dramatizations and
their absolute assurance – here in America –
about what constitutes the good life
(my dead mother still telling me from Miami).
My mother, my tribe.
Strung out on wires
in black and white.
God can forsake them, whenever.
Hasn't He?
He has the option.
I don't.

On Writing

1

When the young hood snarls at him,
Sam Spade says, 'The cheaper the crook,
the gaudier the patter.'
Does this apply to poets?

2

Organize your verse
around a woman –
see Yeats and Dante –
then throw in
the world and death.

3

We file into the chapel
and his verses are read to us in greeting.
Before we file out, his body is wheeled by.
The words of a dead maker prepare to go on trial
through the long seasons of rain and snow.

4

You, lady, leaning down
from the gold bar of heaven,
shine for me over Seventh Avenue,
get me across streets safely,
follow me into dark subways,
remind me of my buried life.

Aubade

As you watch from the bed,
the women rise in their glory
to go to the john. They are
suddenly full-length, dazzling,
the crown of their hair
in the morning light. Bare to their feet
on the wooden floor, moving
as if through a green field,
they bring blue sky into the room
to frame them where they stand
in the immutable space of their being.

How It Ended

1
In the name of love
she sent me to her accountant
who confirmed I was a loser.

2
Because I'm drinking
I think I'm writing
but actually
I'm only drinking.

3
The muse never lets you off the hook.
Tired and sodden, depressed,
whatever, you have to get it up
for her or taste the acid of defeat.

The Defense

1

Will I ever again see
the white implacable Aphrodite?
Maybe on the subway or in the street.

2

And drove the iron tears down Priam's cheek.
Achilles, speaking of his own loss, did that.
White shipping making white wakes on the beaten-metal bay
this clear June day. I sit across from Battery,
the green of its triple arches rising from the water
like the Venice of my imagination.
'It's a universal law,' someone says in passing.
An older voice, rich in surety.
I don't look up, bent over my writing pad,
studying the chaos of my life.

3

Unable to find a cure for death or defense against age,
men remember gigantic actions leading to death,
talk about them, create them again in vividness
as Homer created Troy and its feast for birds.

In Tiberias

Rabbi Akiba
measured the distances
of angels, archangels and principalities
from the throne of God.
It was probably on an August
afternoon like this one,
his beard tangled in calculations,
the noise outside his window –
an old man beating his donkey –
making him aware that angelology
is a refuge like any other.

History

They burned the cities because this life is insupportable.
They killed the Jews because this life is insupportable.
They put on leather and chains and fucked in the streets
because they knew they were animals. Pigs they called the
    others
because they knew *they* were pigs and were searching for
    humans
to kill them too, their books and their buildings.
'He punched her out,' they yelled to each other
and grooved on the slop and the blood.

What It Feels Like

The first night out of Eden
or rather the first morning
after the first night out is
what it always feels like.

I can have a bagel and coffee
but only after I arrive at work.
Until then the despair is too great.
It was different when I woke with you
and prayed to the white curve of your back
and cradled it like the ark of the covenant.

Remembering

Zeros coming out of the sun
plunged me into history.

I was a child of my age,
a warrior. Goodbye to the autonomous life.

When it was quiet and they counted the dead,
I was overcome by despair.

To have been there, and not to be there –
in the blue altitudes, in the cold sun.

Epitaph

Death floats my boat.

Prague

The Gothic half-light
in which moulder
the stones of the Jewish cemetery,
a tumbled mass of stones
crowded on each other
like the cadavers in the camps,
so that you keep sliding out
of one picture into the other.

'The world is a narrow bridge,'
said Rabbi Nachman,
'the important thing
is not to be afraid.'

1949

Memories of Ted Roethke at Yaddo.
He slept beside an inscribed picture of 'Dylie' –
as if they were lovers –
when I came to wake him after my lunch,
and he would rise, vomit,
mix a pitcher of martinis and we
headed for the tennis courts.

Or standing hugely tall in his white suit
at a bar near the track in Saratoga,
he discussed the rival gangs – the
Jarrell gang, for example –
and what we might do to wipe them out.
Or he talked about knocking over a bank
and earning a fellowship. Tall, broody,
drink in hand, king of the rackets.

Or dragging a carton of poetry books
onto the lawn, along with a bottle
of wine kept chilled in the hall refrigerator,
he read for a while, then tried to write.
He asked me once for the lines in Wordsworth
describing a boy racing over a field.

Or reaching back, he told me how
John Crowe Ransom had rejected
'My Papa's Waltz' when it was
submitted to him at the *Kenyon Review*.
And Roethke's eyes filled with tears –
his poem already anthology famous but the wound
open still. The Garden Master but
tendril-tender all his short life.

Choices

He contemplated the bad poetry
he could have written had he
retired to Florida, following
the path his parents had blazed.
He could have described the gulls
winging it over the parking lot,
the thin strip of sand threading the coast
between the poured concrete and the sea.
Friday night bingo and the trailer camps.
Pelicans patrolling the blue-green water.
And the sunsets – drink in hand
standing on the tiny balcony
with the whole fantastic opera
played out in living color.
Or maybe on a party boat out of Haulover,
the Cuban lady of his adolescent dreams,
the lady in red shorts and cap,
could have hooked him hard,
blown him to one last good time,
beached him moneyless and staggering,
with visions in his head and songs to sing.

Hart

His mind had been habituated
to the Vast, living in Brooklyn,
across from the white buildings.

He came upon the heart's
big ecstasy one night
on the IRT

because what else is there
but death.

Generations

In the meridian heat
watching the hummingbird's
air-borne dance, not far
from the blue harp of Kinneret
tilting to my sight
like the tables of the law,
in Galilee, in Jesus country,
near the diner marked 'Loaves and Fishes'
from which I can see
myself in the maze of New York,
following my father's ghost, maybe
with less sense than he
of the promised land.

The Ticket

The poet saw the moon dimglimmering
through the dewy windowpane.
It was a 19th-century moon, soft as moths.
And he was on laudanum or opium.
Only yesterday when I asked her on the phone
why she sounded so happy, she replied:
'I'm on psychopharmaceuticals and in the country.'
Ah, that's the ticket.

Italy, 1996

This Italian earth is special to me
because I was here in a war
when I was young and immortal.
I remember the cypresses in the early morning light
on the road to the airfield
before the sky filled with toiling planes
massing high over Italy for the perilous
crossing to Germany. I remember
on the way back from the target toasting
my frozen cheese sandwich – frozen by the high altitude –
on the electrically-heated casing of my fifty-caliber
machine gun. I remember the taste of life.

Traveling Through Ireland

1
Sitting beside a sign
pointing to Cork and Limerick
or in Irish *Corcaigh*
and *Luimneach*,
I am persuaded again
of my foreignness in this world,
and that none of the signs I read
points to happiness. And
many I can't make out.
Though this world is the only world
it is composed of infinite worlds.
In one of them, I take
my rightful place.

2

On the streets of Donegal
little Irish women
chirping like sparrows
pass tall Viking beauties
astride in black leather.

3

The young woman at the desk
of the Southern Hotel in Sligo
when she heard I was returning
to New York, said appreciatively:
'Ah, the Great Smoke itself.'

4

'It's a long way to Tipperary'
sung at closing time
in a pub in Tipperary
by all assembled –
sorrowfully, joyfully –
explained my life.

5

'Venus could no longer
bear to hear him grieve.'
These words, so lovely in Virgil,
I put beside Austin Clarke's
'Nothing I want to do
can make her frown.'

6

No horseman will pass by my stone.
If I am to be remembered, let it be
by a young woman on the IRT
getting off at Borough Hall.

UNIVERSITY PRESS OF NEW ENGLAND
publishes books under its own imprint and is the publisher for
Brandeis University Press, Dartmouth College, Middlebury
College Press, University of New Hampshire, Tufts University, and
Wesleyan University Press

Library of Congress Cataloging-in-Publication Data

Shapiro, Harvey, 1924–
   [Poems. Selections]
   Selected poems / Harvey Shapiro ; with an introduction by James
Atlas.
      p. cm. — (Wesleyan poetry)
   ISBN 0–8195–2252 X (alk. paper)
   I. Title.   II. Series.
PS3537.H264A6 1997
811'.52—dc21   97–23557